The Wisdom

Translation by
Regis J. Armstrong, O.F.M. Cap., and
Ignatius C. Brady, O.F.M. Cap.
Edited by Doug Fisher

PAULIST PRESS
New York ◆ Mahwah, N.J.

Cover design by Tim McKeen. Cover photo by Don Kimball.

Library of Congress Cataloging-in-Publication Data

Francis, of Assisi, Saint, 1182–1226.
  [Selections. English. 1996]
  True joy : the wisdom of Francis and Clare / translation by Regis J. Armstrong and Ignatius C. Brady ; edited by Doug Fisher.
      p. cm.
  ISBN 0-8091-3672-4 (alk. paper)
    1. Spiritual life—Catholic Church. 2. Joy—Religious aspects—Christianity. 3. Catholic Church—Doctrines. I. Armstrong, Regis J. II. Brady, Ignatius C. III. Fisher, Douglas. IV. Clare, of Assisi, Saint, 1194–1253. V. Title.
BX2179.F64E5 1966
271′.3–dc20   96–12041
                                                                             CIP

Published by Paulist Press
997 Macarthur Boulevard
Mahwah, NJ 07430

Printed and bound in the
United States of America

CONTENTS

INTRODUCTION

*F*rancis has been called everyone's favorite saint. If he is your favorite saint or if you are just curious to find out something about him, this book will enlighten and inspire you. There is much here, too, to learn from Clare, the woman who lived out his wisdom with heroic simplicity.

True Joy: The Wisdom of Francis and Clare contains a selection of the writings attributed to these two spiritual giants. Read this book and catch a glimpse of their vision of the living God.

Saint Francis

THE LIFE OF SAINT FRANCIS

G.K. Chesterton wrote in his reflections on the life of Saint Francis of Assisi: "It is the highest and holiest of the paradoxes that the man who really knows he cannot pay his debt will be forever paying it." No person has ever lived that paradox as fully as the Saint of Assisi, whose vision of the world, its history, and his role in it was characterized by a consciousness of the loving God Who has bestowed on him "every good and perfect gift" (Jas 1:17). Saint Francis spent all his energies attempting to respond to the generosity of God and even as he was dying he exhorted his followers: "Let us begin, brothers, to serve the Lord our God for up to now we have made little or no progress." He was a man overwhelmed by the goodness of a loving God. He was a mystic whose faith had so transformed his vision that he perceived that the entire world was redolent with the power, wisdom, and goodness of the Creator. He was a medieval Italian saint who from the earliest years of his spiritual awakening captured the attention and imagination of men and women of every age and every place. Biographies of Saint Francis of

Assisi exist in almost every language and devotion to him crosses the barriers of all faiths.

Francis was born in the small Umbrian city of Assisi in the year 1181 or 1182 of Pietro de Bernardone, a wealthy textile merchant, and Pica, of a distinguished French family, probably from Picardy. His wealth and love of life made him the leader of Assisi's youth and filled him with dreams of grandeur. In the intercity feuding between Assisi and Perugia he enlisted, entered the battle of Collestrada, and was imprisoned when the troops of Assisi lost. After his release, he returned to Assisi and turned his back on a military career and a promising profession in the business world in order to respond to the impulses of the Lord that moved mysteriously within him. A meeting with a leper and hearing a voice from the cross of San Damiano resulted in his conversion, the renunciation of his possessions, and a project of rebuilding churches.

On February 24, 1208, the feast of Saint Matthias, Francis was working in the little church of Santa Maria degli Angeli, the Portiuncula, and heard the missionary discourse of Matthew's Gospel. He responded immediately and embarked on the life of a poor, itinerant preacher proclaiming a message of penance and peace. Shortly afterward, his first followers joined him and formed a brotherhood dedicated to an intense living of the Gospel life. Within a short period of time, Francis and his brothers set out for Rome to have a simple rule—made up of Gospel texts and a few prescriptions helpful for their common life—approved by Pope Innocent III. This document was approved orally by the Pope. The biographers of the saint tell that Francis also wrote a Gospel plan for sisters (the Poor Ladies of San Damiano), and another for men and women, single and married, who remained in their homes and among their daily secular concerns and strove to live an intense Christian life.

The Spirit of the Gospels impelled Francis to reactivate the Church's missionary activity. He attempted to go to Syria in 1212, but was shipwrecked in Dalmatia. A second journey, to Morocco, was thwarted by his illness in Spain (1213–1214). But in 1219, during the Fifth Crusade, Francis traveled to Damietta, where he tried in vain to convert the Sultan of Egypt, Malik-al-Kamil. During all of these years, however, Francis and his brothers and sisters witnessed and proclaimed the Gospel and became a strong force of renewal in the Church of Europe.

The life of the Poor Man of Assisi is characterized by his total identification with the mysteries of Christ. On December 25, 1223, at Greccio, he further developed the dramatic presentations of the birth of Christ and brought the crib scene into popular spirituality. His biographers tell of his intense devotion to the mystery of the Eucharist, in which Francis saw the Lord of all creation assume poverty and humility each day so that all men and women might be reconciled with God and one another. The crucified Christ, however, absorbed the saint's attention to a great degree so that the last years of his life became caught up in the mystery of the Cross. On September 14, 1224, while Francis was immersed in a long period of prayer, he received the stigmata, which he carried until his death.

During the last years of his life he was blind and seriously ill. Yet this did not deter him from undertaking a series of preaching missions, ministering to the lepers, and relentlessly encouraging his brothers to give themselves to the ideals of the Gospel. Francis died at Santa Maria degli Angeli, the Portiuncula, on October 3, 1226. Less than two years later, on July 16, 1228, he was canonized by Pope Gregory IX. In 1939 he was proclaimed the patron of Italy and in 1980 he was proclaimed patron of ecology by Pope John Paul II.

It may come as a surprise that so many biographies, whether medieval or modern, pass over almost entirely the writings and dictates of Saint Francis. His Rule, Testament, Canticle of Brother Sun, and, perhaps, his well-known story of true and perfect joy are the few excerpts that attract the consistent attention of historians. His actions often spoke louder than his words. He delighted in dramatizing his responses to the actions or thoughts of his brothers or the ideals to which his heart clung. Indeed, the heart of Franciscan spirituality seems to be caught up in the mystery of the human person of Francis and has been transmitted throughout history not only in his own biography but in the lives and stories of so many of his followers. The Poverello left no lengthy Rule or expositions on the spiritual life; he provided no plan for spiritual exercises or methods of prayer. It is simply the person of Francis of Assisi that captures the heart.

Yet to pass over the few writings that he personally composed or the others he dictated is to neglect his deepest thoughts on the Christian life, the relations he developed among his brothers, sisters, and other creatures that came from the hand of God, and the life of poverty and humility that enabled him to embrace the entire world. These few writings of the Saint of Assisi carry "spirit and life," as he himself described them in the words of John's Gospel (Jn 6:63).

One problem that faces the reader of any of the great mystics is that of language. Many great spiritual writers have struggled with expressions of the experience of God, particularly those that have come from their own interior lives, and have fallen back on the ineffable mystery that surrounds these moments. Language becomes for many mystics an impediment, a stumbling block, and, at best, only a tool that leads to the expectancy of an experience of God and not to the experience itself. This is particularly true of Saint Francis of Assisi. The style of his writings is extremely simple and utterly unobtrusive. No other mystic had so intense an encounter with God as that of the Poverello on Mount La Verna. He was marked with the signs of the stigmata and was left unable to speak of what he had experienced. Yet he gave to Brother Leo, his companion during those days on Mount La Verna, a precious relic that indicated the vision of God he enjoyed. "You are holy, Lord, the only God, You do wonders," it proclaims; "You are strong, You are great, You are the most high." The words reveal an utterly simple vision. They never point to themselves but clearly and spontaneously direct our attention to God. The Poverello emerges through his writings as eager to have his readers move quickly beyond himself and his words to the reality of God. Thus his writings are deceptively simple, yet marvelously profound.

THE WRITINGS OF SAINT FRANCIS

THE ADMONITIONS

All of the manuscripts of the thirteenth century contain these twenty-eight admonitions and thus indicate their importance in the early Franciscan tradition. The biographers, especially the Anonymous of Perugia, describe the practice of Saint Francis in "giving admonitions, reprimands, or directives, as he thought best, after he had consulted the Lord" (Anonymous of Perugia, 37). These statements were considered so important, Thomas of Celano indicates, that the saint wanted them written down and kept exactly as he had dictated them (cf. First Life, 82). Moreover, two fourteenth-century commentators on the Franciscan spiritual life, Angelo Clareno and Bartholomew of Pisa, underscore the importance of the Admonitions in providing Saint Francis's doctrine on the spiritual life.

I   The Body of Christ

1. The Lord Jesus says to His disciples: *I am the way, the truth and the life; no one comes to the Father except through me.* 2. *If you had known me, you would also*

have known my Father; and from now on you will know him and have seen him. 3. *Philip says to him: Lord, show us the Father and it is enough for us. Jesus says to him:* 4. *Have I been with you for so long a time and you have not known me? Philip, whoever sees me, sees also my Father* (Jn 14:6–9). 5. *The Father lives in inaccessible light* (cf. 1 Tm 6:16), and *God is Spirit* (Jn 4:24) and, *No one has ever seen God* (Jn 1:18). 6. Therefore He cannot be seen except in the Spirit since *it is the Spirit that gives life; the flesh does not offer anything* (Jn 6:64). 7. But neither, inasmuch as He is equal to the Father, is the Son seen by anyone other than the Father [or] other than the Holy Spirit.

8. Therefore all those who saw the Lord Jesus according to [His] humanity and did not see and believe according to the Spirit and the Godhead that He is the true Son of God were condemned. 9. And now in the same way, all those who see the sacrament [of the Body of Christ], which is sanctified by the words of the Lord upon the altar at the hands of the priest in the form of bread and wine, and who do not see and believe according to the Spirit and the Godhead that it is truly the most holy Body and Blood of our Lord Jesus Christ, are condemned. 10. [This] is attested by the Most High

Himself Who says: *This is my Body and the Blood of my new testament [which will be poured out for many]* (cf. Mk 14:22, 24) 11. and *He who eats my flesh and drinks my blood has eternal life* (cf. Jn 6:55). 12. Therefore it is the Spirit of the Lord, Who lives in His faithful, Who receives the most holy Body and Blood of the Lord. 13. All others who do not share in this same Spirit and who presume to receive Him eat and drink judgment to themselves (cf. 1 Cor 11:29).

14. Therefore, *O sons of men, how long will you be hard of heart?* (Ps 4:3) 15. Why do you not recognize the truth and believe in the Son of God? (cf. Jn 9:35) 16. See, daily He humbles Himself (cf. Phil 2:8) as when He came from *the royal throne* (Wis 18:15) into the womb of the Virgin; 17. daily He comes to us in a humble form; 18. daily He comes down from the bosom of the Father (cf. Jn 1:18) upon the altar in the hands of the priest. 19. And as He appeared to the holy apostles in true flesh, so now He reveals Himself to us in the sacred bread. 20. And as they saw only His flesh by means of their bodily sight, yet believed Him to be God as they contemplated Him with the eyes of faith, 21. so, as we see bread and wine with [our] bodily eyes, we too are to see and firmly believe them to be His most holy Body

and Blood living and true. 22. And in this way the Lord is always with His faithful, as He Himself says: *Behold I am with you even to the end of the world* (cf. Mt 28:20).

II The Evil of Self-Will

1. The Lord said to Adam: Eat of every tree; do not eat of the tree of the knowledge of good and evil (cf. Gn 2:16–17). 2. He was able to eat of every tree of Paradise since he did not sin as long as he did not go against obedience. 3. For the person eats of the tree of the knowledge of good who appropriates to himself his own will and thus exalts himself over the good things which the Lord says and does in him, 4. and thus, through the suggestion of the devil and the transgression of the command, what he eats becomes for him the fruit of the knowledge of evil. 5. Therefore it is necessary that he bear the punishment.

III Perfect Obedience

1. The Lord says in the Gospel: *He who does not renounce everything he possesses cannot be my disciple* (Lk 14:33); 2. and: He *who wishes to save his life must lose it* (Lk 9:24). 3. That person leaves everything he possesses and loses his body who surrenders his whole

self to obedience at the hands of his prelate. 4. And whatever he does and says which he knows is not contrary to his [prelate's] will , provided that what he does is good, is true obedience. 5. And should the subject sometimes see that some things might be better and more useful for his soul than what the prelate may command him, let him willingly offer such things to God as a sacrifice; and instead earnestly try to fulfill the wishes of the prelate. 6. For this is loving obedience because it pleases God and neighbor.

7. But if the prelate should command something contrary to his conscience, although [the subject] does not obey him, still he should not abandon him. 8. And if in consequence he suffers persecution from others, let him love them even more for [the love of] God. 9. For whoever chooses to endure persecution rather than be separated from his brothers truly remains in perfect obedience for he lays down *his life* (Jn 15:13) for his brothers. 10. There are indeed many religious who, under the pretext of seeking something better than what the prelate commands, look back (cf. Lk 9:62) and *return to the vomit* of their own will (cf. Prv 26:11; 2 Pt 2:22); 11. these are murderers who cause many souls to perish by reason of their bad example.

IV Let No One Appropriate to Himself the Role of Being Over Others

1. *I did not come to be served but to serve* (cf. Mt 10:28), says the Lord. 2. Those who are placed over others should glory in such an office only as much as they would were they assigned the task of washing the feet of the brothers. 3. And the more they are upset about their office being taken from them than they would be over the loss of the office of [washing] feet, so much the more do they store up treasures to the peril of their souls (cf. Jn 12:6).

V No One Should Boast in Himself but Rather Glory in the Cross of the Lord

1. Be conscious, O man, of the wondrous state in which the Lord God has placed you, for He created you and formed you to the image of His beloved Son according to the body, and to His likeness according to the spirit (cf. Gn 1:26). 2. And [yet] all the creatures under heaven, each according to its nature, serve, know, and obey their Creator better than you. 3. And even the demons did not crucify Him, but you together with them have crucified Him and crucify Him even now by delighting in vices and sins.

4. In what then can you glory? 5. For if you were so subtle and wise that you had all knowledge (cf. 1 Cor 13:2) and knew how to interpret all tongues (cf. 1 Cor 12:28) and minutely investigate [the course of] the heavenly bodies, in all these things you could not glory, 6. for one demon knew more about the things of earth than all men together, even if there may have been someone who received from the Lord a special knowledge of the highest wisdom. 7. Likewise, even if you were more handsome and richer than everyone else and even if you performed wonders such as driving out demons, all these things would be an obstacle to you and none of them would belong to you nor could you glory in any of these things. 8. But in this we can glory: in our infirmities (cf. 2 Cor 12:5) and bearing daily the holy cross of our Lord Jesus Christ (cf. Lk 14:27).

VI The Imitation of the Lord

1. Let all of us, brothers, look to the Good Shepherd Who suffered the passion of the cross to save His sheep. 2. The sheep of the Lord followed Him in tribulation and persecution, in insult and hunger, in infirmity and temptation, and in everything else, and they have received everlasting life from the Lord because of

18

these things. 3. Therefore, it is a great shame for us, servants of God, that while the saints[actually] did such things, we wish to receive glory and honor by [merely] recounting their deeds.

VII   Good Works Must Follow Knowledge

1. The Apostle says: *The letter kills, but the spirit gives life* (2 Cor 3:6). 2. Those are killed by the letter who merely wish to know the words alone, so that they may be esteemed as wiser than others and be able to acquire great riches to give to [their] relatives and friends. 3. In a similar way, those religious are killed by the letter who do not wish to follow the spirit of Sacred Scripture, but only wish to know [what] the words [are] and [how to] interpret them to others. 4. And these are given life by the spirit of Sacred Scripture who do not refer to themselves any text which they know or seek to know, but, by word and example, return everything to the most high Lord God to Whom every good belongs.

VIII   The Avoidance of the Sin of Envy

1. The Apostle says: *No one can say "Jesus is Lord" except in the Holy Spirit* (1 Cor 12:3); 2. and: *There is no one who does good, not even one* (Rom 3:12). 3. Therefore,

whoever envies his brother the good which the Lord says or does in him commits a sin of blasphemy, because he envies the Most High Who says and does every good (cf. Mt 20:15).

IX   True Love

1. The Lord says: *Love your enemies [do good to those who hate you, and pray for those who persecute and blame you]* (Mt 5:44). 2. That person truly loves his enemy who is not upset at any injury which is done to himself, 3. but out of love for God is disturbed at the sin of the other's soul. 4. And let him show his love for the other by his deeds.

X   The Chastisement of the Body

1. Many people, when they sin or receive an injury, often blame the Enemy or some neighbor. 2. But this is not right, for each one has the [real] enemy in his own power; that is, the body through which he sins. 3. Therefore *blessed is that servant* (Mt 24–46) who, having such an enemy in his power, will always hold him captive and wisely guard himself against him, because as long as he does this, no other enemy, seen or unseen, will be able to harm him.

XI No One Should Be Corrupted by the Evil of Another

1. Nothing should upset the servant of God except sin. 2. And no matter how another person may sin, if the servant of God lets himself become angry and disturbed because of this, [and] not because of love, he stores up the guilt for himself (cf. Rom 2:5). 3. That servant of God who does not become angry or upset at anything lives justly and without anything of his own. 4. And he is blessed who does not keep anything for himself, rendering *to Caesar what is Caesar's, and to God what is God's* (Mt 22:21).

XII How to Discern Whether One Has the Spirit of the Lord

1. A servant of God may be recognized as possessing the Spirit of the Lord in this way: 2. if the flesh does not pride itself when the Lord performs some good through him—since the flesh is always opposed to every good; 3. rather he considers himself the more worthless in his own eyes and esteems himself less than all others.

XIII Patience

1. *Blessed are the peacemakers for they shall be called the children of God* (Mt 5:9). The servant of God cannot

know how much patience and humility he has within himself as long as everything goes well with him. 2. But when the time comes in which those who should do him justice do quite the opposite to him, he has only as much patience and humility as he has on that occasion and no more.

XIV Poverty of Spirit

1. *Blessed are the poor in spirit, for the kingdom of heaven is theirs* (Mt 5:3). 2. There are many who, applying themselves insistently to prayers and good deeds, engage in much abstinence and many mortifications of their bodies, 3. but they are scandalized and quickly roused to anger by a single word which seems injurious to their person, or by some other things which might be taken from them. 4. These [persons] are not poor in spirit because a person who is truly poor in spirit hates himself (cf. Lk 14:26) and loves those who strike him on the cheek (cf. Mt 5:39).

XV Peace

1. *Blessed are the peacemakers, for they shall be called the children of God* (Mt 5:9). 2. The true peacemakers are those who preserve peace of mind and body for

love of our Lord Jesus Christ, despite what they suffer in this world.

XVI   Purity of Heart

1. *Blessed are the pure of heart, for they shall see God* (Mt 5:8). 2. The truly pure of heart are those who despise the things of earth and seek the things of heaven, and who never cease to adore and behold the Lord God living and true with a pure heart and soul.

XVII   The Humble Servant of God

1. *Blessed is that servant* (Mt 24:46) who does not pride himself on the good that the Lord says or does through him any more than on what He says or does through another. 2. That person sins who wishes to receive more from his neighbor than what he is willing to give of himself to the Lord God.

XVIII   Compassion for One's Neighbor

1. Blessed is the person who bears with his neighbor in his weakness to the degree that he would wish to be sustained by him if he were in a similar situation (cf. Gal 6:2; Mt 7:12). 2. Blessed is the servant who attributes every good to the Lord God, for he

who holds back something for himself *hides within himself the money of his Lord God* (Mt 25:18), and *that which* he thought *he had shall be taken away from him* (Lk 8:18).

XIX The Humble Servant of God

1. Blessed is the servant who esteems himself no better when he is praised and exalted by the people than when he is considered worthless, simple, and despicable; 2. for what a man is before God, that he is and nothing more. 3. Woe to that religious who has been placed in a high position by others and does not wish to come down of his own will. 4. And *blessed is that servant* (Mt 24:46) who does not place himself in a high position of his own will and always desires to be under the feet of others.

XX The Good and the Vain Religious

1. Blessed is that religious who takes no pleasure and joy except in the most holy words and deeds of the Lord 2. and with these leads people to the love of God in joy and gladness (cf. Ps 50:10). 3. Woe to that religious who delights in idle and frivolous words and with these provokes people to laughter.

XXI The Frivolous and Talkative Religious

1. Blessed is the servant who, when he speaks, does not reveal everything about himself in the hope of receiving a reward, and who is not quick to speak (cf. Prv 29:20), but wisely weighs what he should say and how he should reply. 2. Woe to that religious who does not keep in his heart the good things the Lord reveals to him (cf. Lk 2:19, 51) and who does not manifest them to others by his actions, but rather seeks to make such good things known by his words. 3. He thereby receives his reward (cf. Mt 6:2, 16) while those who listen to him carry away but little fruit.

XXII Correction

1. Blessed is the servant who would accept correction, accusation, and blame from another as patiently as he would from himself. 2. Blessed is the servant who when he is rebuked quietly agrees, respectfully submits, humbly admits his fault, and willingly makes amends. 3. Blessed is the servant who is not quick to excuse himself and who humbly accepts shame and blame for a sin, even though he did not commit any fault.

XXIII Humility

1. Blessed is the servant who is found to be as humble among his subjects as he would be among his masters. 2. Blessed is the servant who remains always under the rod of correction. He is *the faithful and prudent servant* (Mt 24:45) who for all his offenses does not delay in punishing himself, inwardly through contrition and outwardly through confession and penance for what he did.

XXIV True Love

Blessed is the servant who would love his brother as much when he is sick and cannot repay him as he would when he is well and can repay him.

XXV [The Same Point]

Blessed is the servant who would love and respect his brother as much when he is far from him as he would when he is with him; and who would not say anything behind his back which in charity he could not say to his face.

XXVI The Servants of God Should Honor the Clergy

1. Blessed is the servant who has faith in the clergy who live uprightly according to the norms of the

Roman Church. 2. And woe to those who look down upon them; for even though they may be sinners, nonetheless no one is to judge them since the Lord alone reserves judgment on them to Himself. 3. For inasmuch as their ministry is greater in that it concerns the most holy Body and Blood of our Lord Jesus Christ, which they receive and which they alone administer to others, 4. so those who sin against them commit a greater sin than [if they sinned] against all other people of this world.

XXVII How Virtue Drives Out Vice

1. Where there is charity and wisdom
     there is neither fear nor ignorance.
2. Where there is patience and humility,
     there is neither anger nor disturbance.
3. Where there is poverty with joy,
     there is neither covetousness nor avarice.
4. Where there is inner peace and meditation,
     there is neither anxiousness nor dissipation.
5. Where there is fear of the Lord to guard the house
     (cf. Lk 11:21), there the enemy cannot gain entry.
6. Where there is mercy and discernment,
     there is neither excess nor hardness of heart.

XXVIII *Hiding a Good Thing That It May Not Be Lost*

1. Blessed is that servant who stores up in *heaven* (Mt 6:20) the good things which the Lord has revealed to him and does not desire to reveal them to others in the hope of profiting thereby, 2. for the Most High Himself will manifest His deeds to whomever He wishes. 3. Blessed is the servant who keeps the secrets of the Lord in his heart (cf. Lk 2:19, 51).

THE CANTICLE OF BROTHER SUN

This magnificent hymn expresses the mystical vision of the Saint of Assisi and, since it springs from the depths of his soul, provides us with many insights into the profundity of his life of faith in the Triune God, Who so deeply enters into creation. In this vision, however, the Little Poor Man does not lose himself in space or in the vastness of the created world. He becomes so intimate and familiar with the wonders of creation that he embraces them as "Brother" and "Sister," that is, members of one family. More than any other aspect of the Canticle, this unique feature has enhanced the spiritual tradition of Christian spirituality.

1. Most High, all-powerful, good Lord,
   Yours are the praises, the glory, the honor, and
   all blessing.
2. To You alone, Most High, do they belong,
   and no man is worthy to mention Your name.
3. Praised be You, my Lord, with all your creatures,
   especially Sir Brother Sun,
   Who is the day and through whom You give us
   light.
4. And he is beautiful and radiant with great
   splendor;
   and bears a likeness of You, Most High One.
5. Praised be You, my Lord, through Sister Moon
   and the stars,
   in heaven You formed them clear and precious
   and beautiful.
6. Praised be You, my Lord, through Brother Wind,
   and through the air, cloudy and serene, and
   every kind of weather
   through which You give sustenance to Your
   creatures.
7. Praised be You, my Lord, through Sister Water,
   which is very useful and humble and precious
   and chaste.

8. Praised be You, my Lord, through Brother Fire,
through whom You light the night
and he is beautiful and playful and robust
and strong.

9. Praised be You, my Lord, through our Sister
Mother Earth,
who sustains and governs us,
and who produces varied fruits with colored
flowers and herbs.

10. Praised be You, my Lord, through those who
give pardon for Your love
and bear infirmity and tribulation.

11. Blessed are those who endure in peace
for by You, Most High, they shall be crowned.

12. Praised be You, my Lord, through our Sister
Bodily Death,
from whom no living man can escape.

13. Woe to those who die in mortal sin.
Blessed are those whom death will find in
Your most holy will,
for the second death shall do them no harm.

14. Praise and bless my Lord and give Him thanks
and serve Him with great humility.

THE CANTICLE OF EXHORTATION TO
SAINT CLARE AND HER SISTERS

Francis wrote this canticle in a time when Saint Clare and her sisters, the Poor Ladies of Damiano, needed consolation and encouragement.

1. Listen, little poor ones called by the Lord,
     who have come together from many parts
     and provinces:

2. Live always in truth,
     that you may die in obedience.

3. Do not look at the life outside,
     for that of the Spirit is better.

4. I beg you through great love,
     to use with discretion
     the alms which the Lord gives you.

5. Those who are weighed down by sickness
     and the others who are wearied because of
     them, all of you: bear it in peace.

6. For you will sell this fatigue at a very high price
     and each one [of you] will be crowned queen
     in heaven with the Virgin Mary.

THE EXHORTATION TO THE PRAISE OF GOD

The text of this prayer comes through a manuscript written by the Franciscan historian Marianus of Florence (†1537). The author claims that the prayer was written on a wooden panel that formed an antependium of an altar in the hermitage of Cesi di Terni in Umbria.

1. *Fear the Lord and give Him honor* (Rv 14:7).
2. The Lord is *worthy to receive* praise and honor (Rv 4:11).
3. All you *who fear the Lord praise Him* (cf. Ps 21:24).
4. *Hail Mary, full of grace, the Lord is with you* (Lk 1:28).
5. Heaven and earth, praise Him (cf. Ps 68:35).
6. All you rivers, praise Him (cf. Dn 3:78).
7. *All you children of* God, *bless the Lord* (cf. Dn 3:78).
8. *This is the day which the Lord has made, let us exult and rejoice in it* (Ps 117:24)! Alleluia, alleluia, alleluia! *O King of Israel* (Jn 12:13)!
9. *Let every spirit praise the Lord* (Ps 150:6).
10. *Praise the Lord for He is good* (Ps 146:1); all you who read this, *bless the Lord* (Ps 102:21).

11. All you creatures, bless the Lord (cf. Ps 102:22).
12. *All you birds of the heavens*, praise the Lord
    (cf. Dn 3:80; Ps 148:10).
13. All you *children*, praise the Lord (cf. Ps 112:1).
14. *Young men and virgins*, praise the Lord
    (cf. Ps 148:12).
15. *The Lamb Who was slain is worthy to receive*
    praise, glory and honor (cf. Rv 5:12).
16. Blessed be the holy Trinity and undivided Unity.
17. Saint Michael the Archangel, defend us in battle.

THE LAST WILL WRITTEN FOR SAINT CLARE
AND HER SISTERS

The source of this writing is the Rule of Saint Clare,
*Chapter VI, in which Clare tells of the Seraphic Father's
eagerness to have his followers persevere in the life and
poverty of the Lord Jesus Christ. The work has great signifi-
cance in its witness to the basic ideals that absorbed the
Poverello during the last days of his life. No doubt Saint
Clare placed it in her Rule to encourage her sisters to
embrace a life of poverty in a manner faithful to the teachings of the Poverello.*

1. I, brother Francis, the little one, wish to follow the life and poverty of our most high Lord Jesus Christ and of His most holy mother and to persevere in this until the end; 2. and I ask and counsel you, my ladies, to live always in this most holy life and in poverty. 3. And keep most careful watch that you never depart from this by reason of the teaching or advice of anyone.

THE PARCHMENT GIVEN TO BROTHER LEO

With this brief piece written in his own hand (and now preserved in Assisi at the Basilica of Saint Francis), Francis opens his heart to us, to reveal not only his prayers and meditations on Mount La Verna after the reception of the Stigmata (mid-September 1224), but also his deep love and solicitude for Brother Leo, priest, companion, and scribe.

Side One: The Praises of God

1. *You are* holy, Lord, the only *God, You do wonders.* (Ps 76:15)
2. You are strong, You are great, You are the most high,

You are the almighty King.
You, *Holy Father*, the King *of heaven and earth*.
   (Jn 17:11; Mt 11:25)
3. You are Three and One, Lord God of gods;
      (cf. Ps 135:2)
   You are good, all good, the highest good,
   Lord, God, living and true. (cf. 1 Thes 1:19)
4. You are love, charity.
   You are wisdom; You are humility; You are
      patience; (cf. Ps 70:5)
   You are beauty; You are meekness; You are
      security;
   You are inner peace; You are joy; You are our
      hope and joy;
   You are justice; You are moderation, You are all
      our riches
   [You are enough for us].
5. You are beauty, You are meekness;
   You are the protector, (cf. Ps 30:5)
   You are our guardian and defender:
   You are strength; You are refreshment.
      (cf. Ps 42:2)
6. You are our hope, You are our faith, You are our
      charity,

You are all our sweetness,
You are our eternal life:
Great and wonderful Lord
God almighty, Merciful Savior.

Side Two: A Blessing Given to Brother Leo

1. *May the Lord bless you and keep you;*
   May He show His face to you and be merciful to
   *   you.*
2. *May He turn His countenance to you and give*
   *   you peace (Nm 6:24–26).*
3. *May the Lord bless you, Brother Leo*
   *   (cf. Nm 6:27b).*

PRAISES TO BE SAID AT ALL THE HOURS

The contents of this medley of biblical praises is suffi-
cient to characterize it as coming from the Seraphic
Father, for it is filled with many texts that he uses
throughout his writings. The prayer that concludes the
praises is simply an echo of that prominent image of God
Who is "all good, supreme good, wholly good." This, too,
can be discovered throughout the writings.

1. Holy, holy, holy Lord God Almighty, Who is
   and Who was and
   Who is to come (cf. Rv 4:8):
   Let us praise and glorify Him forever.
2. O Lord our God, You are worthy to receive
   praise and glory and
   honor *and blessing* (cf. Rv 4:11):
   Let us praise and glorify Him forever.
3. The Lamb Who was slain is worthy to receive
   power and divinity,
   and wisdom and strength, and honor and
   glory and blessing (Rv 5:12):
   Let us praise and glorify Him forever.
4. Let us bless the Father and the Son with the
   Holy Spirit:
   Let us praise and glorify Him forever.
5. Bless the Lord, all you works of the Lord
   (Dn 3:57):
   Let us praise and glorify Him forever.
6. Sing praise to our God, all you His servants and
   you who fear God,
   the small and the great (Rv 19:5).
   Let us praise and glorify Him forever.

7. Let heaven and earth praise Him Who is
   glorious (cf. Ps 68:35):
   Let us praise and glorify Him forever.
8. And every creature that is in heaven and on
   earth and under the
   earth and in the sea and those which are in
   them (Rv 5:13):
9. Glory to the Father and to the Son and to the
   Holy Spirit:
   Let us praise and glorify Him forever.
10. As it was in the beginning, is now, and will be
    forever. Amen.
    Let us praise and glorify Him forever.
11. Prayer:

All-powerful, most Holy,
most high, and supreme God:
all good,
supreme good,
You Who *alone are good*;
may we give You
all praise, all *glory*,
all thanks, all *honor:*
all *blessing*,
and all good things.

So be it.
So be it.
Amen.

THE SALUTATION OF THE VIRTUES

*The more one ponders this simple text, the more Saint
Francis is revealed as a theologian of the workings of the
Spirit and of divine grace in the soul of one who has sur-
rendered himself entirely to God by "dying" to self to live
totally for God.*

*The work can be divided into three major sections: the
salutations addressed to the virtues, the dispositions necessary for their reception, and the description of each
one's activity. The consideration of each of the virtues in
a feminine sense is an expression of the medieval milieu
from which this writing comes. What is curious, though,
is the manner of linking certain virtues to one another.
The combination established between wisdom and simplicity, poverty and humility, and love and obedience
speak eloquently of the unique vision of Saint Francis.*

1. Hail, Queen Wisdom, may the Lord protect you
   with your sister, holy pure Simplicity.

2. Lady, holy Poverty, may the Lord protect you
   with your sister, holy Humility.
3. Lady, holy Charity, may the Lord protect you
   with your sister, holy Obedience.
4. O most holy Virtues, may the Lord protect all
   of you,
   from Whom you come and proceed.
5. There is surely no one in the entire world
   who can possess any one of you
   unless he dies first.
6. Whoever possesses one [of you]
   and does not offend the others,
   possesses all.
7. And whoever offends one [of you]
   does not possess any
   and offends all.
8. And each one destroys vices and sins.
9. Holy, Wisdom destroys
   Satan and all his subtlety.
10. Pure holy Simplicity destroys
    all the wisdom of this world
    and the wisdom of the body.
11. Holy Poverty destroys
    the desires of riches

and avarice
and the cares of this world.

12. Holy Humility destroys pride
and all the people who are in the world
and all things that belong to the world.

13. Holy Charity destroys
every temptation of the devil and of the
flesh and every carnal fear.

14. Holy Obedience destroys
every wish of the body and of the flesh

15. and binds its mortified body
to obedience of the Spirit
and to obedience of one's brother

16. and [the person who possesses her] is subject
and submissive
to all persons in the world

17. and not to man only
but even to all beasts and wild animals

18. so that they may do whatever they
want with him
inasmuch as it has been given to them
from above by the Lord.

THE PRAYER INSPIRED BY THE OUR FATHER

In the Middle Ages meditation on each phrase of the Lord's Prayer was quite common. Saint Francis may have borrowed heavily from other writings in this prayer, but in many ways this Prayer Inspired by the Our Father *is an expression of the inner life of Saint Francis.*

1. O OUR most holy FATHER,
   Our Creator, Redeemer, Consoler, and Savior

2. WHO ARE IN HEAVEN:
   In the angels and in the saints,
   Enlightening them to love, because You, Lord, are light
   Inflaming them to love, because You, Lord, are love
   Dwelling [in them] and filling them with happiness,
      because You, Lord, are the Supreme Good,
         the Eternal Good
         from Whom comes all good
         without Whom there is no good.

3. HALLOWED BE YOUR NAME:
   May our knowledge of You become ever clearer

That we may know the breadth of Your
        blessings
  the length of Your promises
  the height of Your majesty
  the depth of Your judgments

4. YOUR KINGDOM COME:
So that You may rule in us through Your grace
and enable us to come to Your kingdom
  where there is an unclouded vision of You
    a perfect love of You
    a blessed companionship with You
    an eternal enjoyment of You

5. YOUR WILL BE DONE ON EARTH AS IT IS IN
HEAVEN:
That we may love You with our whole heart by
        always thinking of You
  with our whole soul by always desiring You
  with our whole mind by directing all our
    intentions to You and by seeking Your
    glory in everything
  and with our whole strength by spending all
      our energies and affections
      of soul and body
      in the service of Your love

and of nothing else
and may we love our neighbors as ourselves
> by drawing them all with our whole strength
> to Your love
>
> by rejoicing in the good fortunes of others
> as well as our own
>
> and by sympathizing with the misfortunes of
> others
>
> and by giving offense to no one

6. GIVE US THIS DAY:
in memory and understanding and reverence
> of the love which [our Lord Jesus Christ] had
> for us
>
> and of those things which He said and did
> and suffered for us

OUR DAILY BREAD:
Your own Beloved Son, our Lord Jesus Christ

7. AND FORGIVE US OUR TRESPASSES:
Through Your ineffable mercy
through the power of the Passion of Your
Beloved Son
> together with the merits and intercession of
> the Blessed Virgin
> Mary and all Your chosen ones

8. AS WE FORGIVE THOSE WHO TRESPASS
   AGAINST US:
   And whatever we do not forgive perfectly,
   do You, Lord, enable us to forgive to the full
   so that we may truly love [our] enemies
   and fervently intercede for them before You
   returning no one evil for evil
   and striving to help everyone in You
9. AND LEAD US NOT INTO TEMPTATION
   Hidden or obvious
   Sudden or persistent
10. BUT DELIVER US FROM EVIL
    Past, present, and to come.

Glory to the Father and to the Son and to the Holy
Spirit
As it was in the beginning, is now, and will be for-
ever. Amen.

TRUE AND PERFECT JOY

*This description of perfect joy graphically portrays
Saint Francis's understanding of true minority and
expresses the Franciscan ideal through the medium of the
human person.*

1. [Brother Leonard] related, in the same place [the Portiuncula], that one day at Saint Mary the blessed Saint Francis called Brother Leo and said: "Brother Leo, write!" 2. He answered: "I'm ready." 3. "Write," [Francis] said, "what true joy is:

4. "A messenger comes and says that all the masters in Paris have come into the Order; write: this is not true joy. 5. Or that all the prelates beyond the mountains [have entered the Order], as well as the archbishops and bishops; or, that the king of France and the king of England [have entered the Order]; write: this is not true joy. 6. Again, that my brothers have gone to the nonbelievers and converted all of them to the faith; again, that I have so much from God that I heal the sick and perform many miracles: I tell you that true joy does not consist in any of these things."

7. "What then is true joy?"

8. "I return from Perugia and arrive here in the dead of night; and it is winter time, muddy and so cold that icicles have formed on the edges of my habit and keep striking my legs, and blood flows from such wounds. 9. And all covered with mud and cold, I come to the gate and after I have knocked and called for some time, a brother comes and asks: 'Who are you?' I

answer: 'Brother Francis.' 10. And he says: 'Go away; this is not a proper hour for going about; you may not come in.' 11. And when I insist, he answers: 'Go away, you are a simple and a stupid person; we are so many and we have no need of you. You are certainly not coming to us at this hour!' 12. And I stand again at the door and say: 'For the love of God, take me in tonight.' 13. And he answers: 'I will not. 14. Go to the Crosier's place and ask there.' 15. I tell you this: If I had patience and did not become upset, there would be true joy in this and true virtue and the salvation of the soul."

Saint Clare

THE LIFE OF SAINT CLARE

*S*ome sixty years after her birth, Pope Alexander IV proclaimed Clare of Assisi a saint of the universal Church and rhapsodized on her name:

> O Clare, endowed with so many titles of clarity! Clear (*clara*) even before your conversion, clearer (*clarior*) in your manner of living, exceedingly clear (*praeclarior*) in your enclosed life, and brilliant (*clarissima*) in splendor after the course of your mortal life. In Clare, a clear mirror is given to the entire world.

This papal bull of canonization, *Clara claris praeclara*, captures the unique place of the most dedicated follower of the Poor Man of Assisi by poetically expressing the symbolic dimension of her life. Clare of Assisi, one of the great women of the Christian and Franciscan tradition, is a translucent statement of the spiritual reality of life. "A clear mirror," as the Pope calls her, so that whoever gazes into her writings will discover a reflection of the glory of God and the beauty of the human person.

In the opening paragraphs of the *Legend of Saint Clare*, written shortly after her canonization in 1255, the author describes the apprehension of Ortolana, the saint's mother, as the time of her child's birth drew near. She frequently visited a nearby church, the account narrates, and one day heard a response to her prayer for the safe delivery of her child. "O lady," the voice told her, "do not be afraid, for you will joyfully bring forth a clear light which will illumine the world." Within a short time, a female child was born to Ortolana and her husband, Favarone, and was named Chiara or Clare, the clear one.

Clare was the third of five children born to this somewhat well-to-do family of Assisi. The *Legend* does not hesitate in describing her as a holy, dedicated young woman even before her "conversion." "The Spirit worked within and formed her into a most pure vessel," her biographer writes of her childhood, so that "she began to be praised by her neighbors...and the report of her goodness was noised about among the townspeople." Docility to her parents, generosity and compassion for the poor, dedication to daily prayer: These are some of the virtues Clare's biographer lists among the qualities of her youth.

It is difficult to determine when Clare first met Francis, the popular young man who had turned his back on the military establishment and the business world, but she probably heard him proclaim his message of penance and peace in the piazzas of Assisi. It is certainly possible that Clare may have heard the young Francis preach in the cathedral of San Rufino in 1210, for her family lived directly across from it. At about this time her uncle made arrangements for her to marry Ranieri de Bernardo, but Clare refused and, with the help of her servant, Bona di Guelfuccio, made arrangements to meet Francis and receive his advice. "The Father Francis," the *Legend* narrates, "exhorted her to contempt of the world, vividly showing her how vain was earthly hope, how deceptive worldly beauty. He manifested to her the sweetness of the nuptials of Christ and persuaded her to keep the pearl of her virginal purity for that blessed Bridegroom Whom love made Man." On Palm Sunday, March 18, 1212, Clare followed the advice of the Poverello, accepted a palm branch (the symbol of martyrdom) from the bishop of Assisi, and on the following evening went to the Portiuncula, where Francis received her commitment to follow him in the pursuit of Gospel perfection.

Saint Francis and the friars escorted Clare to the Benedictine nuns in the monastery of San Paolo in Bastia, a short distance from Santa Maria degli Angeli (the Portiuncula) until more definite provisions could be provided. Then, after her relatives attempted to persuade her to return to her former way of life, the Seraphic Father moved her to the monastery of San Angelo di Panzo and, finally, to San Damiano, the first of the little churches the young Francis had repaired. Clare remained in that same dwelling for forty-two years, that is, until her death in 1253. Within a short period of time the young woman was joined by others, including her younger sister Agnes, and the "Poor Ladies" of Assisi became recognized as followers of the Poor Man of Assisi.

In her Rule, Clare provides a short "form of life" that the Seraphic Father gave to her and her sisters. It is a simple statement, which describes the Trinitarian foundations of the life at San Damiano, as well as the close ties that Saint Francis saw binding the Poor Ladies and the friars. Although there are no other documents of either Francis or Clare that provide more details concerning the daily life of the sisters, Thomas of Celano, in his *First Life of Saint Francis* (c. 1228), presents a beautiful description of the community at San Damiano. The opening sentence of these paragraphs suggests the reticence of later authors in examining in detail the manner of living followed by the Poor Ladies:

> Over her [Clare] arose a noble structure of most precious pearls, whose *praise is not from men but from God* (Rom 2:29), since neither is our limited understanding sufficient to imagine it, nor our scanty vocabulary to utter it.

Yet Celano proceeds to praise Clare and her sisters for the steadfast practice of charity, humility, virginity and chastity, poverty, abstinence and silence, patience, and contemplation. What is remarkable about these paragraphs is their composition during the lifetime of Clare herself, who would have heard them read with each celebration of the Feast of Saint Francis.

The development of the Poor Ladies, however, must be seen against the background of the Fourth Lateran Council (1215) and its legislation forbidding the establishment of any new religious orders. By the time of the council, Clare and her sisters had become recognized as a religious community, but there is no evidence indicating papal approbation for their way of life. Thus the prescription of the council directly affected the form of life followed by the Poor Ladies of San Damiano.

As the fame of the San Damiano foundation began to spread and new monasteries were established, the Cardinal Deacon, Hugolino, was appointed their protector from 1218 to 1219. In order to provide a more stable form of living for Clare and her sisters, Hugolino provided a new, detailed, and austere Rule that was based on the Benedictine Rule. Two most important points, however, were clearly missing from this Rule: the pursuit of radical poverty and dependence on the Order of Friars Minor. Thus a struggle began for Clare that was to continue throughout her entire life. The saint desired to write her own Rule based on that of the Friars Minor in which the pursuit of evangelical perfection and poverty would form a firm foundation.

Within a year of Hugolino's election as the bishop of Rome, the new Pope Gregory IX followed the example of his predecessor, Pope Innocent III, and acceded to the wishes of Clare for a special privilege to practice poverty. The papal document, *Sicut manifestum est,* September 17, 1228, permitted the sisters to live in perfect poverty and to reject the possession of any goods.

On August 6, 1247, Pope Innocent IV provided a new Rule for all the monasteries of the Poor Ladies and in a papal bull, *Quoties a nobis*, August 23, 1247, bound them to its observance. This second Rule was a milder form of that given by Hugolino and even allowed common ownership of movable and immovable goods. The Pope declared in another papal bull, *Inter Personas*, July 6, 1250, that no sister could be forced to accept this Rule and so it lost its binding force. At about this time, Clare began to write her own Rule based on that of Saint Francis and accepted the minor details of the Rules of Hugolino and Innocent IV.

Throughout all these years of struggle, Clare was ill and confined to bed. The *Legend* speaks of her continual illness during a span of twenty-eight years, yet it does not provide any clues as to the nature of her malady. The Process of Canonization indicates that the extreme mortification and rigorous penance of Clare's life took a severe toll on her health. Nonetheless, Clare appears as a strong, determined woman who was convinced of the charism of poverty that she had received through the Seraphic Father and was insistent on obtaining papal approval in order to protect it for ages to come.

In September 1252, Cardinal Raynaldus, the Cardinal Archbishop of Ostia and Velletri and, therefore, the Protector of the Poor Ladies, visited the sickbed of Clare and approved her Rule with the following words:

> Beloved daughters in Christ, because you have rejected the splendors and pleasures of the world and, *following the footprints* (1 Pt 2:21) of Christ Himself and of His most holy Mother, you have chosen to live in the cloister and to serve the Lord in highest poverty so that, in freedom of soul, you may be the Lord's servants, We approve your holy way of life in the Lord and with fatherly affection we desire to freely impart our benign favor to your wishes and holy desires.

But this approval did not satisfy Clare, who continued to seek the approval of Pope Innocent IV. She had to wait for almost eleven more months before the papal bull *Solet annuere*, August 9, 1253, put her at ease.

Two days later, August 11, 1253, Clare died, and was buried in the church of San Giorgio where Saint Francis had been placed before his body was transferred to the basilica built in his honor. The body of Clare still remains there, although it is now honored by another basilica of Assisi, which is dedicated to her memory.

A frequent representation of Clare of Assisi depicts her holding a monstrance containing the Eucharist and, through her devotion, putting to flight the Saracens who threatened San Damiano. That image may well symbolize Clare's entire life, for it epitomizes her strong, courageous faith, which struggled against and overcame the prudence of the world. Thirty-four of the forty-one years of Clare's life at San Damiano were spent in a determined effort to preserve the purity of the Franciscan ideal of poverty. From this perspective Clare is a vital part of the Franciscan heritage and the transmission of the spirit of the Poverello was achieved through her determination. Indeed, when this "little plant of the most blessed Father Francis," as she calls herself, is seen against the background of the history of the Franciscan Family between 1226, the year of the death of Saint Francis, and 1253, the year of Saint Clare's own death, it is not difficult to envision the loss of the great ideal of radical, evangelical poverty. While the friars were accepting papal indults that relaxed their practice of poverty, Clare was courageously clinging to the primitive ideals and challenging the Holy See to allow her and her sisters to maintain the charism of poverty, which she had received from Francis himself.

Through this woman, then, the Spirit of the Lord expressed the Franciscan ideal in a pure, brilliant way and confronted and challenged her contemporaries to a serious consideration of its value. Her very name, Clare, expresses her position as a clear and clarifying expression of the spirituality of the Poor Man of Assisi.

The Spirituality of Saint Clare

Within seven years of Saint Clare's death another great follower of the Poor Man of Assisi, the Seraphic Doctor Saint Bonaventure, was wrestling with the articulation of the unique vision of the Franciscan tradition. After two years as Minister General of the Friars and Protector or the Poor Ladies of Saint Clare, he went to La Verna in order to discover peace and from that place of the profound mystical experience of Saint Francis, Saint Bonaventure wrote to the Poor Ladies of Assisi asking them for their prayers. A sentence in that letter expresses perfectly the relationship and the position of Francis and Clare in the tradition of Christian spirituality: "May you walk earnestly in the footprints of your holy Mother (Clare) who, through the instrumentality of the little poor man Saint Francis, was schooled by the Holy Spirit."

It is only through an understanding of divine power of the Holy Spirit that the total unanimity of these great saints of Assisi can be brought into proper perspective. Moved by divine inspiration, they became perfect symbols of the presence of that Spirit which leads us to the Inner Life of the Father and the Son and challenges us to a profound love of one another and of the gifts of creation.

It cannot be denied, however, that Clare as a woman and as a dedicated student of the Seraphic Father Francis expressed his spiritual vision in a unique way. Her femininity expressed the universal validity of the charism of Saint Francis and accentuated its rich and enduring qualities. As a most eager and attentive student, Clare learned from her teacher, Francis, and brought his teachings to new audiences. Her great contribution to the Franciscan tradition consists in her untiring defense of the charism of poverty, which she had received from the Poverello and which was challenged by the prudent of the world. Clare of Assisi became a most important means of the transmission of the Franciscan spirit at a time when the powerful presence of the Seraphic Father was missed by all of his followers.

In order to best determine the unique gifts of Clare to the Franciscan tradition, a comparison of her Rule with the *Later Rule* of Saint Francis should be studied in detail. Three prominent differences are immediately noticed: (1) the practice of a material separation from the world, that is, the enclosure; (2) the total permeation of daily life with the pursuit of radical poverty; and (3) the struggle to preserve "the unity of mutual love and peace" as a means of achieving sanctification. It cannot be denied that all of these elements can be discovered in the writings of the Seraphic Father, but they are prominent in that document of Clare which was challenged by the Holy See. Thus they provide an opportunity of examining Clare's vision of the Franciscan tradition as she acquired it from Saint Francis and passed it on to her own followers.

The Material Separation from the World

It is difficult to determine when the legislation obliging the Poor Ladies of San Damiano to live an enclosed life was actually given to them. At the beginning of the thirteenth century, women who embraced the religious life were generally obliged to live separated from the world. Clare was no exception to this. A careful examination of the documents indicates that from the earliest days San Damiano was a place of strict enclosure where Clare, on entering, enclosed herself and where there were nuns who lived in the same cloister and did not leave it during the forty-two years of Clare's life. No doubt the first prescriptions were promulgated in the Rule of Cardinal Hugolino di Segni in 1218 or 1219. But it is important to consider that Clare, who was strong enough to challenge the Pope when he proposed a way of life in contrast to her profound convictions and her ideal of gospel perfection, accepted a Rule that embraced a strict enclosure. In fact, Clare introduced into her own Rule of 1253 the practice of the enclosure, which she had observed from the beginning of her religious life, as well as the same norms of the Rule of Hugolino. This point was underscored by Cardinal Raynaldus, the Cardinal Protector of the Poor Ladies, in his letter of introduction to the Rule of Clare as he recognized her resolution "to live in the cloister and to serve the Lord in highest poverty."

Throughout the history of religious life a theology of the enclosure had gradually developed. Those early men and women of the desert discovered that the undoing of the sin of Adam was best achieved by the embrace of a life of obedience, that is, by the submission of the will to that of another person who represented God. The cenobitic life, which valued this virtue of obedience so highly, gradually conceived the monastery as a microcosm of the world in which a "new paradise" could be developed and in which the contemplative state of the first human being could be restored. Thus the monks and nuns of the monastic world developed art, architecture, music, and the literature of the Greek and Roman worlds as part of their spiritual environment. Yet such a view of the religious world that was eager to develop an atmosphere through objects of beauty and transcendence frequently overlooked the spiritual realities that were at the heart of such a perspective.

Clare was heir to this theology of the monastic world and, as a woman of the early thirteenth century, knew of many of the struggles of the religious of the previous century to return to the purity of the vision of their founders. She no doubt took the enclosure as a matter of course and in so doing she purified the monastic tradition of this most enervating force: the acceptance of movable and immovable goods. For the cloistered world of the Poor Ladies was characterized by the renunciation of every illusion, of every attraction and expectation, that was not rooted in God from Whom every good comes. The new paradise of Clare was a return to the poverty of the Garden of Eden as the anonymous author of the *Sacrum Commercium sancti Francisci cum Domina Paupertate*, written in 1227, had described it through the words of Lady Poverty.

I was at one time *in the paradise of my God* (Rv 2:7), where man went naked; in fact I walked in man and with man in his nakedness through the whole of that most splendid paradise, fearing nothing, doubting nothing, and suspecting no evil. It was in my thoughts that I would be with him forever, for he was created just, good, and wise by the Most High and placed in that most pleasant and most beautiful place. I was rejoicing exceedingly and *playing before him all the while* (Prv 8:30), for, possessing nothing, he belonged entirely to God.

History placed Clare in the very first place in the struggle for the defense of that Franciscan poverty and gave to her words a vibrant and passionate resonance that the norms prescribing the enclosure do not have. But this does not mean that she did not value the cloister as a necessary element of her religious life and that of her sisters. Quite the contrary; the life of the "poor enclosed nuns of the Order of Saint Mary of San Damiano," as Hugolino referred to them in his Rule, injected into the theology of the enclosure a new element: the embrace of a life of radical poverty.

The Total Permeation of Life with Poverty

From this perspective, it is understandable that Clare could so easily write to Blessed Agnes of Prague and encourage her to leave the pleasures of an earthly kingdom and to embrace a religious life that was separated materially from the world. The monastic enclosure of the Poor Ladies, as it was seen by Clare, provided the setting for the building of the kingdom of heaven in which eternal riches, glory, and honor were lavishly given by God. The *First Letter to Blessed Agnes of Prague* clearly reveals Clare's indefatigable faith in the words of Jesus: "Blessed are the poor in spirit, for the kingdom of heaven is theirs" (Mt 5:3). She writes:

O blessed poverty
   who bestows eternal riches on those who love
   and embrace her!
O holy poverty
   to those who possess and desire you
   God promises the *kingdom of heaven*
   and offers indeed eternal glory and blessed life.

And again:

> Contempt of the world has pleased You more
> than [its] honors, poverty more than earthly
> riches, and You have stored up greater *treasures in*
> *heaven* rather than on earth, *where rust does not*
> *consume nor moth destroy nor thieves break in and*
> *steal* (Mt 6:20). Your reward, then, is very great in
> heaven (Mt 5:12)!

This conviction is even more emphatically stated as
Clare reminds Agnes: "You know, I am sure, that the
Kingdom of heaven is promised and given by the Lord
only to the poor" (cf. Mt 5:3).

A curious difference between the writings of
Francis and those of Clare is the emphasis given to
poverty. For Francis, the total obedience of Christ to

the will of His Father prompted Him not to cling to what was rightfully His but to empty Himself (cf. Phil 2:6–11). Thus Saint Francis wrote more on the practice of obedience than on that of poverty. On the other hand, Clare insisted on the importance of poverty so strongly because she always kept her attention fixed on the "poor" Christ. Since mankind was "spiritually" poor and deprived of eternal values, Christ made Himself "physically" poor and helpless, in order to bring spiritual riches and to enable man to gain possession of the kingdom of heaven. The spiritual life, then, consists of conforming oneself to the poor Christ by the observance of the most perfect poverty. By living in poverty, Clare maintains, she and her sisters chose to enter upon the "narrow" way that leads to the kingdom of heaven.

Throughout her Rule, Clare repeatedly accentuates the poverty of Christ. It is a basic prerequisite for entrance into the Order, expressed in the manner of dress; forms the foundation for the life described by Saint Francis for them; and is the means by which union with God and with one another is achieved and maintained. Even a superficial examination of the Rule of Saint Clare reveals how thoroughly poverty permeates the entire life of the community of San Damiano. Clare certainly manifests a profound appreciation of the charism of Saint Francis and its importance for his followers' way to God.

This dedication to poverty is beautifully expressed in the papal Privilege of Poverty, which Pope Gregory IX gave to Clare on 17 September 1228:

> As is manifest, in the desire to dedicate yourselves to the Lord alone you have renounced all desire for temporal things; wherefore you have sold all things and given them to the poor and propose to have no possessions whatever, that in all things you may cleave to the footprints of Him Who became for us the Way, the Truth and the Life. (Jn 14:6)
>
> Nor does the lack of possessions deter you from such a proposal; for the left hand of the heavenly Bridegroom is under your head (cf. Sg 2:6; 8:3) to support what is weak in your body which you have subordinated to the law of your mind and brought into subjection.
>
> Finally, He Who feeds the birds of the air and the lilies of the field will not fail you in both food and vesture, until He Himself comes and

serves you (Lk 12:37) in eternity, when namely His right hand will embrace you in the fullness of His vision.

As you have thus petitioned us, so we confirm by Apostolic favor your proposal of highest poverty.

The Struggle to Preserve the Unity of Mutual Love

This poverty, so highly praised by Pope Gregory IX, provides for Clare a capacity for God and an openness to His Presence. It takes on a "sacramental" quality in that it is an outward expression of a much deeper reality, a poverty in which the human person comes to know his only real possessions: his vices and sins. Thus this pursuit of radical poverty is integrally tied to the contemplative ideal as well as to the community life embraced by Clare and her sisters in the enclosure of San Damiano. The repetition of the concepts "holy unity" and "highest poverty" that are expressed in the introductions of Pope Innocent IV and Cardinal Raynaldus to the *Rule of Saint Clare* underscores the connection between these aspects of religious life.

At the heart of these concepts is the presence of the

Spirit of the Lord, Who establishes the basic relationships of the spiritual life. In his *First Letter to the Faithful*, Francis states that the Spirit of the Lord rests on those who embrace a life of penance and makes them "children of the heavenly Father...spouses, brothers, and mothers of Our Lord Jesus Christ." Clare echoes this theme in her *First Letter to Agnes of Prague*, but perceives poverty as the tool that opens the human person to these divine relationships. In a beautiful way, Clare gently leads Agnes to cherish her new familial and marital status, which the choice of religious life had intensified for her, and encourages her to a deeper poverty because of it. Thus the *Second Letter to Agnes of Prague* becomes a medley of the two themes of poverty and contemplation, of clinging "*to the footprints* (1 Pt 2:21) of Him to Whom you have merited to be joined as a Spouse."

More than any other follower of the Poor Man of Assisi, Clare emerges as a poor, contemplative woman. Her letters definitely reveal these elements of her life and provide insights into the means she chose to intensify them. "Believing nothing, agreeing with nothing which would dissuade you from this resolution," she writes to Agnes, "...so that you may offer your vows to the Most High in the pursuit of that perfection to which the Spirit of the Lord has called you." "As a poor virgin embrace the poor Christ. Look upon Him...gaze upon [Him], consider [Him], contemplate Him, as you desire to imitate Him." The result of these efforts is a magnificent Christology that focuses on the revelation of God that is found in Jesus and takes the Trinitarian spirituality of Francis a step further. Whereas Francis seems to be struggling always with that broken relationship with Pietro Bernardone, his earthly father, by accentuating the spiritual relationship with his heavenly Father, Clare appears to embrace God Who has revealed Himself as a loving Son and Spouse and chose poverty in order to make us rich.

There is a continual struggle or desire in the writings of Clare to preserve that bond of unity which the Spirit of the Lord has established in her life with God. If poverty emerges as the prerequisite for establishing her relationships with God, Father, Son, and Holy Spirit, then contemplation is the peace-filled enjoyment of them as well as the means to live more intensely the charism of that way which Francis shows.

Yet there is a further dimension that appears in the *Rule of Saint Clare*. It is also the overflow of the poverty and spiritual life articulated in the letters to Blessed Agnes of Prague. This is the intense life of community that the Spirit brings to Clare and her sisters and that is accentuated more strenuously than in the *Later Rule of Saint Francis*. "Let them be ever zealous to preserve among themselves the unity of mutual love," Clare writes in Chapter X, "which is the bond of perfection."

Once more the gift of brotherhood and sisterhood is brought before the followers of the Poor Man of Assisi. More than a community of support, the sisters are seen as a means of salvation in manifesting the profound relationships that exist in the Inner Life of God. No more beautiful expression of this aspect of the spiritual life of Clare can be discovered than in the *Fourth Letter to Blessed Agnes of Prague*:

> Let the tongue of the flesh be silent when I seek to express my love for you; and let the tongue of the Spirit speak because the love I have for you, O blessed daughter, can never be fully expressed by the tongue of the flesh, and even what I have written is an inadequate expression.

The genius of Clare's perception of the spiritual life can be seen in this aspect of her Rule, for she penetrated, as

Francis did, the marvelous mystery of the Revelation of God Who reveals Himself as a Community of Love. There can be little doubt that the enclosed life of San Damiano struggled on a daily basis to express that Unity of God.

Conclusion

Many contemporary biographers of Saint Francis imaginatively romanticized his relationship with a woman who became one of his most devoted followers: Clare of Assisi. These authors, building on the meager facts of the early biographical tradition, tend to overshadow her important role in the Franciscan tradition. Through this woman the Spirit of the Lord expressed the Franciscan ideal in a pure, brilliant manner and challenged her contemporaries to a serious consideration of its value in the history of the Church.

It is impossible to imagine the reason for Clare's birth in the early part of the thirteenth century when women were obliged to live religious life in the enclosure. If Clare had lived a few centuries later, she might well have been a dynamic woman who proclaimed the Gospel through an active, apostolic life. Yet the mystery of God's Providence has placed her in the annals of history as a stable, translucent symbol of the vision of Saint Francis of Assisi. Her long life at San Damiano expresses in a unique way the heart of the dynamism of Saint Francis, who heard the call to rebuild the church as he knelt in prayer before the crucifix of that small chapel.

The followers of Saint Clare, living in poor, enclosed communities throughout the world, have continued that tradition. While the friars have been moving throughout the world witnessing, proclaiming, and suffering for the Gospel, these noble women have remained stable, unassuming beacons of the poverty and contemplation that are at the heart of the Franciscan Ideal. The person of Clare epitomizes their call: to be clear and clarifying expressions of the Spirit of the Lord, Who works in the hearts of all men and women in hidden and mysterious ways.

THE WRITINGS OF SAINT CLARE

THE TESTAMENT OF SAINT CLARE

*T*his text forms a beautiful autobiographical reflec-
*tion of Saint Clare. No other writing of the saint—
with the exception of the sixth chapter of her Rule—speaks
so eloquently about the origins of the Poor Ladies of San
Damiano, the bond of unity between the Poor Ladies and
Saint Francis and his brothers, the love of poverty and
humility that is the life of the "Little Flock" raised up by
the Father to follow the footprints of Christ in the
Church. Yet the* Testament of Saint Clare *is certainly one
of the most controversial texts in that its authenticity has
been frequently brought into doubt. Nonetheless, it is a
magnificent source of the spirituality of Saint Clare from
which many valuable insights can be gained.*

In the name of the Lord!
1. Among all the other gifts which we have received
and continue to receive daily from our benefactor, *the
Father of mercies* (2 Cor 1:3), and for which we must
express the deepest thanks to our glorious God, our
vocation is a great gift. Since it is the more perfect and

greater, we should be so much more thankful to Him for it. For this reason the Apostle writes: "Acknowledge your calling" (1 Cor 1:26). 2. The Son of God became for us *the Way* (cf. Jn 14:6) which our Blessed Father Francis, His true lover and imitator, has shown and taught us by word and example.

3. Therefore, beloved Sisters, we must consider the immense gifts which God has bestowed on us, especially those which He has seen fit to work in us through His beloved servant, our blessed Father Francis, not only after our conversion but also while we were still [living among] the vanities of the world.

4. For, almost immediately after his conversion, while he had neither brothers nor companions, when he was building the Church of San Damiano in which he was totally filled with divine consolation, he was led to abandon the world completely. This holy man, in the great joy and enlightenment of the Holy Spirit, made a prophecy about us which the Lord fulfilled later. Climbing the wall of that church he shouted in French to some poor people who were standing nearby: "Come and help me build the monastery of San Damiano, because ladies will dwell here who will

glorify our heavenly Father throughout His holy Church by their celebrated and holy manner of life."

5. In this, then, we can consider the abundant kindness of God toward us. Because of His mercy and love, He saw fit to speak these words about our vocation and selection through His saint. And our most blessed Father prophesied not only for us, but also for those who were to come to this [same] holy vocation to which the Lord has called us.

6. With what solicitude and fervor of mind and body, therefore, must we keep the commandments of our God and Father, so that, with the help of the Lord, we may return to Him an increase of His *talents* (cf. Mt 25:15–23). For the Lord Himself not only has set us as an example and mirror for others, but also for our [own] sisters whom the Lord has called to our way of life, so that they in turn will be a mirror and example to those living in the world. Since, therefore, the Lord has called us to such great things, that those who are to be models and mirrors for others may behold themselves in us, we are truly bound to bless and praise the Lord and to be strengthened constantly in Him to do good. Therefore, if we have lived according to the form [of

life] given us, we shall, by very little effort, leave others a noble example and gain the prize of eternal happiness.

7. After the most high heavenly Father saw fit in His mercy and grace to enlighten my heart to do penance according to the example and teaching of our most blessed Father Francis, shortly after his own conversion, I, together with the few sisters whom the Lord had given me soon after my conversion, voluntarily promised him obedience, since the Lord had given us the Light of His grace through his holy life and teaching.

8. But when the Blessed Francis saw that, although we were physically weak and frail, we did not shirk deprivation, poverty, hard work, distress, or the shame or contempt of the world—rather, as he and his brothers often saw for themselves, we considered [all such trials] as great delights after the example of the saints and their brothers—he rejoiced greatly in the Lord. And moved by compassion for us, he promised to have always, both through himself and through his Order, the same loving care and special solicitude for us as for his own brothers.

9. And thus, by the will of God and our most blessed Father Francis, we went to dwell at the Church of San Damiano. There, in a short time, the Lord

increased our number by His mercy and grace so that what He had predicted through His saint might be fulfilled. We had stayed in another place [before this], but only for a little while.

10. Later on he wrote a form of life for us, [indicating] especially that we should persevere always in holy poverty. And while he was living, he was not content to encourage us by many words and examples to love and observe holy poverty; [in addition] he also gave us many writings so that, after his death, we should in no way turn away from it. [In a similar way] the Son of God never wished to abandon this holy poverty while He lived in the world, and our most blessed Father Francis, following His footprints, never departed, either in example or teaching, from this holy poverty which he had chosen for himself and for his brothers.

11. Therefore, I, Clare, the handmaid of Christ and of the Poor Sisters of the Monastery of San Damiano—although unworthy—and the little plant of the holy Father, considered together with my sisters our most high profession and the command of so great a father. [We also take note] in some [sisters] of the frailty which we feared in ourselves after the death of our holy Father Francis, [He] who was our pillar of strength

and, after God, our one consolation and support. [Thus] time and again, we bound ourselves to our Lady, most holy Poverty, so that, after my death, the Sisters present and to come would never abandon her.

12. And, as I have always been most zealous and solicitous to observe and to have the other sisters observe the holy poverty which we have promised the Lord and our holy Father Francis, so, too, the others who will succeed me in office should be bound always to observe it and have it observed by the other sisters. And, for even greater security, I took care to have our profession of most holy poverty, which we promised our Father [Francis], strengthened with privileges by the Lord Pope Innocent, during whose pontificate we had our beginning, and by his other successors. [We did this] so that we would never nor in any way depart from it.

13. For this reason, on bended knees and with all possible respect, I commend all my sisters, both those present and those to come, to our holy Mother the Church of Rome, to the supreme Pontiff, and especially to the Lord Cardinal who has been appointed [Protector] for the Order of Friars Minor and for us. [Inspired by] the love of the Lord Who was poor as He lay in the crib, poor as He lived in the world, Who

remained naked on the cross, may [our Protector] always see to it that his *little flock* (cf. Lk 12:32) observe that which [our] Lord [and] Father has begotten in His holy Church by the word and example of our blessed Father Francis, who followed the poverty and humility of His beloved Son and His glorious Virgin Mother— namely, holy poverty, which we have promised God and our most blessed Father Francis. May he always encourage and support them in these things.

14. The Lord gave us our most blessed Father Francis as Founder, Planter, and Helper in the service of Christ and in the things we have promised to God and to himself as our father. While was living he was always solicitous in word and in deed to cherish and take care of us, his little plant. For these reasons I commend my sisters, both those present and those to come, to the successor of our blessed Father Francis and to the entire Order, so that they may always help us to progress in serving God more perfectly and above all to observe most holy poverty in a more perfect manner.

15. If these sisters should ever leave this place and go elsewhere, after my death, wherever they may be, they are bound nonetheless to observe that form of poverty which we have promised God and our most blessed

Father Francis. 16. Nonetheless, let both the sister who is in office and the other sisters exercise such care and farsightedness that they do not acquire or receive more land around the place than strict necessity requires for a vegetable garden. But if, for the integrity and privacy of the monastery, it becomes necessary to have more land beyond the limits of the garden, no more should be acquired than strict necessity demands. This land should not be cultivated or planted but always remain untouched and undeveloped.

17. In the Lord Jesus Christ, I admonish and exhort all my sisters, both those present and those to come, to strive always to imitate the way of holy simplicity, humility, and poverty and [to preserve] the integrity of [our] holy manner of life, as we were taught by our blessed Father Francis from the beginning of our conversion to Christ. Thus may they always remain *in the fragrance* of a good name (cf. 2 Cor 2:15), both among those who are afar off and those who are near. [This will take place] not by our own merits but solely by the mercy and grace of our Benefactor, *the Father of mercies* (cf. 2 Cor 1:3).

18. Loving one another with the charity of Christ, let the love you have in your hearts be shown out-

wardly in your deeds so that, compelled by such an example, the sisters may always grow in love of God and in charity for one another.

19. I also beg that sister who will have the office [of caring for] the sisters to strive to exceed others more by her virtues and holy life than by her office so that, encouraged by her example, the sisters may obey her not so much out of duty but rather out of love. Let her also be prudent and attentive to her sisters just as a good mother is to her daughters; and especially, let her take care to provide for them according to the needs of each one from the things which the Lord shall give. Let her also be so kind and so available that all [of them] may reveal their needs with trust and have recourse to her at any hour with confidence as they see fit, both for her sake and that of her sisters.

20. But the sisters who are subjects should keep in mind that for the Lord's sake they have given up their own wills. Therefore I ask that they obey their mother as they have promised the Lord of their own free will so that, seeing the charity, humility, and unity they have toward one another, their mother might bear all the burdens of her office more lightly. Thus what is

painful and bitter might be turned into sweetness for her because of their holy way of life.

21. And because the way and path is straight and the gate through which one passes and enters into life is narrow (cf. Mt 7:14), there are few who walk on it and enter through it. And if there are some who walk that way for a time, there are very few who persevere in it. How blessed are those to whom it has been given to walk that way and persevere to the end!

22. Therefore, as we have set out on the path of the Lord, let us take care that we do not turn away from it by our own fault or negligence or ignorance nor that we offend so great a Lord and His Virgin Mother, and our Father, the blessed Francis, and the Church Triumphant and, indeed, the Church Militant. For it is written: *"Cursed are those who turn away from Your commandments"* (Ps 118:21).

23. *For this reason I bend my knees to the Father of our Lord Jesus Christ* (Eph 3:14), that through the prayers and merits of the glorious and holy Virgin Mary, His Mother, and of our most blessed Father Francis and all the Saints, the Lord Himself Who has given us a good beginning will [also] give the increase and constant perseverance to the end. Amen.

24. So that it may be observed better, I leave this writing for you, my dearest and most beloved Sisters, those present and those to come, as a sign of the blessing of the Lord and of our most blessed Father Francis and of my blessing—I who am your mother and servant.

THE BLESSING ATTRIBUTED TO SAINT CLARE

The Legend of Saint Clare, 45, portrays the last hour of the saint's earthly life. As she was dying, Clare blessed her sisters at San Damiano, as well as those in other monasteries and those who would come in the future.

1. In the name of the Father and of the Son and of the Holy Spirit. Amen.

2. May the Lord bless you and keep you. 3. May He show His face to you and be merciful to you. 4. May He turn His countenance to you and give you peace.

5. I, Clare, a handmaid of Christ, a little plant of our holy Father Francis, a sister and mother of you and the other Poor Sisters, although unworthy, 6. ask our Lord Jesus Christ through His mercy and through the intercession of His most holy Mother Mary, of Blessed Michael the Archangel and all the holy angels of God,

and of all His men and women saints, 7. that the heavenly Father give you and confirm for you this most holy blessing in heaven and on earth. 8. On earth, may He increase [His] grace and virtues among His servants and handmaids of His Church Militant. 9. In heaven, may He exalt and glorify you in His Church Triumphant among all His men and women saints.

10. I bless you in my life and after my death as much as I can and more than I can 11. with all the blessings with which the Father of mercies has and will have blessed His sons and daughters in heaven and on earth. Amen.

12. Always be lovers of God and your souls and the souls of your Sisters, and always be eager to observe what you have promised the Lord.

13. May the Lord be with you always and, wherever you are, may you be with Him always. Amen.

OTHER BOOKS IN THE SERIES

CREATION AND CHRIST:
THE WISDOM OF HILDEGARD OF BINGEN

THE LIFE OF THE SOUL:
THE WISDOM OF JULIAN OF NORWICH

EVERYTHING AS DIVINE:
THE WISDOM OF MEISTER ECKHART